The Montgomery
Bus Boycott

Frank Walsh

WORLD ALMANAC® LIBRARY

Please visit our web site at: www.worldalmanaclibrary.com
For a free color catalog describing World Almanac® Library's list of high-quality
books and multimedia programs, call 1-800-848-2928 (USA) or 1-800-387-3178
(Canada). World Almanac® Library's fax: (414) 332-3567.

Library of Congress Cataloging-in-Publication Data

Walsh, Frank.
    The Montgomery bus boycott / by Frank Walsh.
      p. cm. — (Landmark events in American history)
    Includes bibliographical references and index.
    Summary: Describes how the black community of Montgomery, Alabama,
staged the 1955 boycott to end segregation on public buses and discusses that
struggle in the context of the Civil Rights Movement.
    ISBN 0-8368-5375-X (lib. bdg.)
    ISBN 0-8368-5403-9 (softcover)
    1. Montgomery (Ala.)—Race relations—Juvenile literature. 2. Segregation
in transportation—Alabama—Montgomery—History—20th century—Juvenile
literature. 3. African Americans—Civil rights—Alabama—Montgomery—History—
20th century—Juvenile literature. [1. Montgomery (Ala.)—Race relations.
2. Segregation in transportation—History. 3. African Americans—Civil rights—
History.] I. Title. II. Series.
F334.M79N484   2003
323.1'196073076147—dc21   2002036020

First published in 2003 by
World Almanac® Library
330 West Olive Street, Suite 100
Milwaukee, WI 53212 USA

Copyright © 2003 by World Almanac® Library.

Produced by Discovery Books
Editor: Sabrina Crewe
Designer and page production: Sabine Beaupré
Photo researcher: Sabrina Crewe
Maps and diagrams: Stefan Chabluk
World Almanac® Library editorial direction: Mark J. Sachner
World Almanac® Library art direction: Tammy Gruenewald
World Almanac® Library production: Jessica Yanke

Photo credits: Alabama Department of Archives and History/Montgomery Advertiser:
p. 26; Corbis: cover, pp. 4, 5, 7, 8, (both), 9, 11, 12, 13, 14, 15, 17, 18, 19 (both),
21, 22, 24, 25, 28, 30, 32, 33, 34, 36, 37, 39, 40, 42, 43; Henry Ford Museum and
Greenfield Village: pp. 20, 23, 29; Library of Congress: pp. 6, 16, 27, 35, 38, 41;
Rosa Parks Museum and Library, Troy State University: p. 31.

Printed in the United States of America

1 2 3 4 5 6 7 8 9 07 06 05 04 03

Contents

Introduction

Montgomery, Alabama

Montgomery is the capital of Alabama, but it was not the first city to have that title. In fact, the capital of Alabama was changed four times before Montgomery was chosen in 1847. It seems only appropriate, however, that Montgomery should be the state capital. This is because a state capital is, among other things, a place where important events occur and landmark decisions are made.

The City of Montgomery

Montgomery is located almost exactly in the center of Alabama and covers a land area of about 135 square miles (350 square kilometers). As of the year 2000, the population of the city was a little over 220,000.

Montgomery is famous for many things, including being the site of the first electric streetcar system, established in 1886. It was in Montgomery that the Wright Brothers founded the first civilian flying school in 1910. Montgomery was also the site chosen for Air University—the education arm of the Air Force—that opened in 1946.

The State Capitol building in Montgomery, Alabama.

Segregation was a part of U.S. society, especially in the South, until the 1960s. It was not just about what drinking fountain you could drink from. Black people had fewer opportunities than whites in work, education, and housing.

The Montgomery Bus Boycott

About fifty years ago, Montgomery was the location of one of the most important events in American history. On December 1, 1955, a black woman named Rosa Parks refused the order of a bus driver to give up her seat to a white passenger on a Montgomery public bus. As a result, Parks was arrested and, in protest, a **boycott** was organized. For over a year, all African Americans refused to use the Montgomery bus system. The boycott ended only when the **Supreme Court** made a decision that **segregation** on buses was **unconstitutional**.

The Montgomery bus boycott was a very significant event for several reasons. It was, in many respects, the beginning of the African-American **civil rights** movement. It was also a springboard for the extraordinary leadership of Dr. Martin Luther King, Jr. Apart from everything else, the story of the Montgomery bus boycott is a remarkable example of courage and determination that continues to inspire people to this very day.

Trampled by Oppression

"There comes a time when people get tired of being trampled over by the iron feet of oppression. . . . I want it to be known that we're going to work with grim and bold determination to gain justice on buses in this city. And we are not wrong. . . . If we are wrong, the Supreme Court of this nation is wrong. If we are wrong, God Almighty is wrong. . . . If we are wrong, justice is a lie."

Martin Luther King, Jr.,
Montgomery, Alabama,
December 5, 1955

Slavery in America

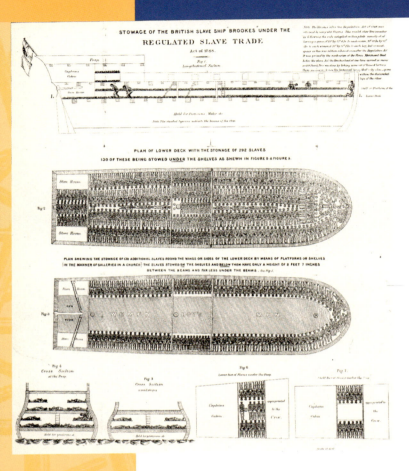

The Origins of Slavery

The United States was not the only country in which slavery was practiced. It was in North America, however, that slavery became identified with race. This is because most of the slaves in colonial America were black people brought from Africa to work for white people.

Indentured Servants

Many white people coming to the British colonies in the 1600s and early 1700s were **indentured** servants, people who had pledged their services in exchange for the cost of their passage to America. They were expected to work for a required amount of time and then they would be set free. Once liberated, former servants were given "freedom dues," which usually included a small plot of land, farming tools, clothing, and sometimes a gun.

In 1619, a Dutch trader brought a small group of Africans to the **colony** of Virginia and exchanged the people for food. This was the first time that Africans were brought to America and sold as laborers.

At first, Africans brought to America were also considered indentured servants. Indentured servitude, however, began to lose favor as the flow of white servants from England decreased in the late 1600s. Another reason slavery became popular was that replacing servants was expensive. It was preferable to own people as slaves, particularly since their children would also be slaves.

This diagram shows a British slave ship that took Africans to North America in the 1790s to be sold as slaves. It carried 454 people, stowed according to the patterns shown here to fit in as many bodies as possible.

Slaves were property, legally owned just like furniture or cattle. Every year in Montgomery, an auction was held where white people could buy, sell, or hire slaves. This drawing shows that auction in 1861.

Slavery Becomes an Institution

In 1641, Massachusetts became the first colony to recognize slavery as a legal institution. One by one, the other colonies continued this process of acceptance. In 1750, Georgia—the last free colony—legalized slavery. By the time of the American Revolution in 1776, therefore, slavery was legal in all of the thirteen colonies. Even Thomas Jefferson—writer of the Declaration of Independence and author of the famous phrase "all men are created equal"—kept slaves. Slavery was a fact of life in the United States from the moment the nation began.

Slavery as a Fact of Life

Slavery became not just a basic part of American life but also of the **economy**, particularly in the South. Throughout the 1700s and until the mid-1800s, slaves were such an essential part of the workforce that Southerners could not contemplate a nation without slavery. Most slaves farmed cotton, tobacco, and other crops on southern plantations.

Speaking Out
"Slavery is such an atrocious debasement of human nature, that its very [abolition], if not performed with solicitous care, may sometimes open a source of serious evils."

Benjamin Franklin, an early speaker against slavery, November 9, 1789

The Abolitionists

Sojourner Truth

Frederick Douglass

Long before civil rights became a movement, there were people who fought for the civil rights of slaves in America. They were known as "abolitionists" because their aim was to abolish slavery.

One of the first was **William Lloyd Garrison** (1805–1879), who founded the American Antislavery Society in 1835. For thirty-five years from 1831, Garrison published and edited a newspaper called the *Liberator*. He was frequently attacked by white people in the North and the South for his beliefs and words.

Sojourner Truth (1797–1883) gained her freedom from slavery in 1828 and became a Christian preacher. In 1843, believing she had been called by God to fight for the rights of slaves and women, she became a lecturer for the abolitionist cause, drawing large crowds. After the Civil War, Truth worked to help freed slaves in Virginia and Washington, D.C.

Another leading abolitionist was **Frederick Douglass** (1817–1896), a slave until his escape in 1838. He became known as a great speaker for the abolition movement and edited the *North Star* abolitionist newspaper from 1847 to 1864. After the Civil War, Douglass worked for the U.S. government both in Washington, D.C., and in the Caribbean.

A group of slaves, including children, leave the cotton field at the end of a working day. Because of slave labor, cotton farming in the South was very profitable for white slave owners.

Many white people opposed slavery, but it would take time before their voices were heard. In the meantime, African slaves suffered harsh working conditions and were beaten frequently, even killed. They were considered less than people. Slaves were the property of their owners, and they were expected to live without any of the rights or dignity of free people.

The Split Between North and South

By the mid-1800s, life—and business especially—differed greatly between the northern and southern United States. The northern states had developed a mostly industrial economy based around factories. And by the early 1800s, slavery had been abolished nearly everywhere in the North. The South, meanwhile, was primarily a farming economy. Cotton, in particular, was the livelihood of the southern states, and slaves made up most of the labor force that produced the cotton. By 1860, there were more than 3.5 million slaves in the South.

Tensions began to rise in the 1840s and 1850s, when the northern states sought to prohibit slavery in the western **U.S. Territories**. The southern states didn't like this because they thought it meant that their right to keep slaves would be taken away. The breaking point came in 1860, when Abraham Lincoln was elected president. Lincoln was part of the newly formed Republican Party, which opposed slavery.

The Civil War Begins

Eleven southern states **seceded** from the **Union**. In February 1861, they formed a new nation, with its own government, called the Confederate States of America. The United States government declared that the southern states had no right to rebel. If they used force against the United States, President Lincoln warned, they would be committing treason, and this would not be permitted. The Confederacy chose to ignore this warning, and the first shots of the Civil War were fired in South Carolina on April 12, 1861.

The Union and the Confederacy

The Union comprised twenty anti-slavery states, most of them in the North. It also included Delaware, Kentucky, Maryland, and Missouri. Known as "border states," these were states where slavery had not been banned but that stayed loyal to the United States. Eleven southern, pro-slavery states formed the Confederate States of America, or the Confederacy. For a brief time, the capital of the Confederacy was Montgomery, Alabama.

KEY
- Union states
- Confederate states
- Border states (Union)
- United States territories

The Emancipation Proclamation

On January 1, 1863, President Lincoln issued the **Emancipation** Proclamation. This declared that all slaves in Confederate states were free. Enforcing this decree, however, was dependent on the Union winning the war. It was four long and bloody years before the Confederacy surrendered on April 9, 1865, and the Civil War was over. Meanwhile, about 600,000 people had died and another million people were seriously injured.

In December 1865, slavery was officially abolished in the United States by the Thirteenth **Amendment** to the U.S. Constitution. This Amendment, however, did not mean that blacks in America would now have an easy life. African Americans finally had their freedom on paper. In the real world, however, things were different.

A painting celebrates the end of slavery by showing Lincoln, on horseback, holding the Emancipation Proclamation. The woman in the carriage is a symbol of freedom.

The End of Slavery

"We shout for joy that we live to recall this righteous moment. . . . 'Free forever' oh! Long enslaved millions, . . . the hour of your deliverance draws nigh! . . . Ye millions of free and loyal men . . . , lift up your voices with joy and thanksgiving for with freedom to the slave will come peace and safety to your country."

Frederick Douglass, abolitionist, in response to the Emancipation Proclamation

11

Segregation and Racism

After the Civil War, life for blacks in America remained in some ways as difficult as it had always been. In a few ways, it was actually worse. This was because freedom from slavery did not mean equality for African Americans. The power and money in the United States still rested with white Americans.

Racist Policies

In southern states, "Black Codes" were introduced after the Civil War. These were laws that forced African Americans into a state of unofficial slavery. They made sure black Southerners continued to provide cheap labor for white people. If a black man was unemployed, he could be arrested. Black Codes also regulated the ways in which black people were allowed to interact with whites. African Americans were to stand at attention and remove their hats when whites passed them on the street. Black Codes also restricted the rights of African Americans to own certain kinds of property. Blacks were not allowed to vote or own guns.

After slavery was abolished, some white people made sure black people did not achieve equality. "Regulators" in the South, unofficial law enforcers such as these men beating a former slave, used violence to punish anyone who stepped out of line.

The Ku Klux Klan

A group of southern men, many of them Confederate army veterans, formed the Ku Klux Klan (KKK) in Pulaski, Tennessee, around 1865. The movement soon spread across the South. KKK members believed in white superiority. They had several goals, including preventing blacks from voting and from getting jobs and good housing. Frequently, the KKK resorted to terrorism and violence to achieve these ends. Members of the KKK carried burning crosses as their symbol. They wore white hooded robes in order to remain anonymous and to frighten their victims.

A Little Progress

There were forces for change and progress, however. The period after the Civil War was known as **Reconstruction**, and some groups both inside and outside of government brought about **reforms** in spite of **racist** policies. A few African Americans were elected to Congress. Black people began to play significant roles in state and local affairs and used their newly gained right to vote to elect Republicans to office. Congress sent federal troops to the South to protect the rights of black citizens.

The End of Reconstruction

By the mid-1870s, however, the Democrats were back in power in the South. Over the years, the Southern states managed to erode the few rights gained by black citizens during Reconstruction. They deprived African Americans of the right to vote by introducing regulations requiring them to read and write or to own property. Most black people did not qualify, and so they were barred from voting.

Jim Crow

By the 1890s, a society based on slavery had evolved into one based on segregation. Blacks and whites in the South—and, to an extent, in the North also—were kept apart in such a way that made it impossible for black people to gain the basic rights or opportunities that would make them equal.

In the late 1800s, the most popular form of entertainment in the United States was the minstrel show. The shows were staged by singing, dancing, white performers wearing black makeup on their faces. One of the minstrels, Thomas Dartmouth "Daddy" Rice, invented a character called Jim Crow, who was a foolish black slave. Eventually, the term "Jim Crow" came to mean the segregation that all blacks experienced in the South.

A cartoon of the character Jim Crow depicts him as a ragged and irresponsible person. He was symbol of inequality and segregation in the South.

JIM CROW,

Separate but Equal

Segregation soon received official recognition. In June 1892, a shoemaker named Homer Plessy boarded a train in New Orleans. Although Plessy appeared white, his great-grandmother had been black. Plessy sat in the white car of the train and refused to move to the blacks-only car, a decision that landed him in jail. Plessy sued the railroad in a **lawsuit** that went all the way to the Supreme Court. In the 1896 case *Plessy v. Ferguson* (Ferguson was the judge in the original district court case), the Supreme Court ruled that separation of races was acceptable as long as "separate but equal" accommodations were made for blacks. This decision confirmed that segregation between blacks and whites would continue in the United States for many years to come.

14

Living Under Segregation

By the 1900s, segregation was common, especially in the southern United States. Transportation, restaurants, theaters, swimming pools, beaches, hotels—public facilities either barred black people or offered them separate facilities. Of course, segregated facilities were rarely equal.

African Americans were prevented from exercising their rights as free citizens in other ways. There were restrictions on where they lived and what jobs they could hold.

There were also some unwritten laws known to everyone in the South. Black people had to behave in a certain way to white people. They were not permitted to look them in the eye. They had to speak respectfully even though whites could speak disrespectfully to them. Any violation of the unwritten rules was likely to lead to physical abuse, and blacks were certainly not allowed to fight back.

Lynching

One terrifying form of cruelty that appeared in the South was lynching, the torturing and killing—typically by hanging—of a person or small group of people by a large mob. Lynching was an especially vicious way for racist white people to express hatred for black people now that they could no longer enslave them. This form of terrorism continued well into the middle of the 1900s.

In the 1930s, every time a black person was lynched, this banner was hung outside the NAACP's offices in New York City. The NAACP continued to call public attention to racist violence and inequality until things began to change.

Strange Fruit

"Southern trees bear strange fruit,
Blood on the leaves and blood at the root,
Black bodies swinging in the Southern breeze,
Strange fruit hanging from the poplar trees. . . .

"Here is a fruit for the crows to pluck,
For the rain to gather, for the wind to suck,
For the sun to rot, for the trees to drop,
Here is a strange and bitter crop."

"Strange Fruit," a song about lynching, written in 1938 by Abel Meeropol (Lewis Allen) and popularized by singer Billie Holiday

A New Century

In the first half of the twentieth century, in spite of all the prejudice and actions of white people, African Americans made progress in organization and education. On February 12, 1909, the National Association for the Advancement of Colored People (NAACP) was founded by a group of **activists**. The NAACP began many years of fighting for change by addressing social injustice in the courts.

One of the most glaring examples of such injustice was in education. In the early 1950s, racial segregation in public schools was a fact of life across the United States. In Topeka, Kansas, a black third-grader named Linda Brown had to walk one mile (1.6 kilometers) through a railroad switchyard every day to get to her black elementary school. This angered her father, Reverend Oliver Brown, because there was a white elementary school only seven blocks from their home. Oliver tried to enroll his daughter in the white elementary school, but its principal refused.

Brown v. Board of Education

With the help of the NAACP, Reverend Brown and a group of thirteen parents filed a **class action** lawsuit against the Board of Education of Topeka. This lawsuit was heard in the U.S. District Court for the District of Kansas in June 1951. The court ruled that no laws were being broken.

The story of *Brown v. Board of Education of Topeka* was not over, however. NAACP lawyers took it to the Supreme Court. The Supreme Court is the most powerful court in the United States because it has **jurisdiction** over all other courts in the nation. A victory in the Supreme Court means victory across the whole nation.

The Supreme Court trial began in December 1852. It took a long time. One of the lawyers at the trial, Thurgood Marshall, argued that school segregation gave black children the message that they were inferior.

NAACP lawyer Thurgood Marshall, center, stands in front of the Supreme Court after winning an historic victory in the case *Brown v. Board of Education of Topeka*. With him are fellow attorneys George Hayes (left) and James Nabrit (right). Marshall later became the first African-American justice appointed to the Supreme Court.

An Important Decision

The trial continued until May 17, 1954, when the Supreme Court ruled that its earlier "separate but equal" ruling was unconstitutional. The Supreme Court decision was a major victory in the struggle for civil rights. It would be the first of many. Slowly, a change was beginning to take place in the South.

The Backlash

After the *Brown v. Board of Education* verdict, however, there was a new sense of danger in the South. The Supreme Court's ruling on the *Brown* case angered many white people. Some whites even referred to the date of the ruling as "Black Monday." The Supreme Court itself was partly to blame for this anger. The Court had made a decision but gave no clear instructions on how it was to be carried out. The Court only advised that school districts act with "all deliberate speed" to **desegregate**. As a result, only two southern states, Texas and Arkansas, began desegregation in 1954.

When African Americans went to Europe as servicemen in World War II in the 1940s, they were fighting for the freedom of people in other countries even though they did not experience it at home. Some found that they were accepted as equals in Europe, and this gave rise to an awareness of their own civil rights.

18

The Case of Emmett Till

Emmett Till

The atmosphere of racial hatred in the South reached its peak in August 1955 with the killing of Emmett Till. Emmett was a fourteen-year-old black child from Chicago visiting relatives in Money, Mississippi. Being from a northern city, he was not used to the status of blacks in the South. During his visit, Emmett was challenged by some local boys to go into a convenience store and speak to a white woman who had just gone inside. Emmett went into the store, bought some candy, and, on his way out, said, "Bye, baby" to the white woman. Three days later, Emmett was taken from his relatives' home and killed.

Mose Wright, one of the relatives with whom Emmett had been staying, testified against the two white men accused of the murder. It was one of the first times that a black man in the South had risked testifying against a white man. The men were not convicted, however. The "not guilty" verdict shocked people, and the story made headlines all over the world.

The all-white jury at the murder trial. Whatever the facts of a case, Southern juries would generally not convict a white man of a crime against a black person during segregation.

Chapter 3

The Spark

The Montgomery Bus System

Like many large American cities in the 1950s, Montgomery had a public bus system. It was run by a company named Montgomery City Bus Lines. The fronts of the buses were for whites only and the backs were for black people. And if a bus was crowded, blacks had to give up their seats so that white people could sit down.

The bus yard of Montgomery City Bus Lines in the 1950s. As with most public facilities, the buses were segregated.

The majority (nearly 75 percent) of the passengers were black. Blacks and other poor people in the 1950s did not usually own cars, and most depended on the bus system for work and shopping.

All of the bus drivers were white, and some were cruel and abusive toward the black passengers. One opportunity for abuse arose because blacks were not allowed to board the bus at the front. After entering at the front to pay their fare, black passengers had to step off the bus and reenter through the back door. Often, the driver would pull away after people had paid their fares, leaving them stranded. Sometimes, the drivers would shout abuse at black passengers, calling them names like "ape" or using other racist insults.

Edward D. Nixon

Edward D. Nixon was one of the people leading the movement for desegregation of public facilities. Nixon was convinced that a boycott of the bus system in Montgomery would be effective, but only if he found the right person to be the center of the movement. In order to be a figurehead for the protest, the person would need to have the right kind of image.

Claudette Colvin and Mary Louise Smith were two black people who had previously refused to give up their seats for white passengers. Nixon decided, however, that neither of the women would be a suitable figurehead for the movement. He waited. As Nixon later said, "I had to be sure that I had somebody I could win with."

December 1, 1955

On the evening of December 1, 1955, a tailor's assistant named Rosa Parks left her job at a Montgomery department store and waited at a bus stop for a ride home. Parks had experienced the humiliation of inequality and racism on the buses before. In fact, when she boarded the bus that night, she recognized the driver, James Blake. On a rainy night some twelve years before, Blake had ordered Parks to get on his bus using the rear entrance. When Parks stepped off the bus to come in through the back door, Blake had driven away, leaving her to walk home in the rain.

Edward D. Nixon, seen (left) with Rosa Parks, was a long-time activist and former president of the Alabama NAACP. In 1955, he was hoping for an opportunity to lead a boycott of the Montgomery buses to protest segregation.

As Good as Any White Person
"I said I was just as good as any white person and I wasn't going to get up. . . . I was crying then, I was very hurt because I didn't know that white people could act like that."

Claudette Colvin, testifying in a Montgomery federal court, May 11, 1956

Rosa Parks (born 1913)

Rosa Parks at the ceremony awarding her the Congressional Gold Medal in 1999.

Rosa Parks was born Rosa McCauley in Tuskegee, Alabama. She grew up in the small town of Pine Level near Montgomery. As small children, Rosa and her brother went to a segregated rural school. At the age of eleven, Rosa entered the Montgomery Industrial School for Girls, and as a teenager she went on to the Booker T. Washington Junior High School. She left school before graduating to care for her family.

In 1932, Rosa married a Montgomery barber named Raymond Parks, who was a member of the NAACP. She was soon actively involved in civil rights, and in 1943 she became secretary of the Montgomery chapter of the NAACP.

In 1955, by refusing to be a victim of racism, Rosa Parks became the heroine that the civil rights movement needed. After the bus boycott ended, however, both Rosa and Raymond Parks lost their jobs and were threatened with violence. The couple moved to Detroit, where they struggled for several years to find employment. In 1965, Rosa Parks was hired by Congressman John Conyers and worked in his office until she retired in 1988. She has received numerous awards for her tireless efforts on behalf of civil rights: the NAACP's Spingarn Medal (1970), the Martin Luther King, Jr. Award (1980), the Presidential Medal of Freedom (1996), and the Congressional Gold Medal (1999).

Rosa Parks was sitting at the front of the black people's section on this bus when she refused to give up her seat. The bus is now in the Henry Ford Museum.

The night in December 1955, however, Parks did get on board. The bus was already crowded, and at the next stop even more passengers boarded. The driver ordered the blacks who were sitting to give up their seats for the white riders. Although she had not planned to do so, Rosa Parks refused to move. Blake threatened to call the police and have Parks arrested. Parks replied, "You may do that."

Parks Is Arrested

Rosa Parks was arrested for defying local and state laws requiring segregation in buses. She was taken to the city jail, where police took her picture and fingerprints. Parks was released but told to come to court on the following Monday. She was later convicted of violating segregation laws and fined $10 plus $4 in court costs.

Dignity and Self-Respect

"What I learned best at Miss White's school [Montgomery Industrial School for Girls] was that I was a person with dignity and self-respect, and I should not set my sights lower than anybody else just because I was black."

Rosa Parks, writing about her experience at the school for African-American girls she attended in 1924, Rosa Parks: My Story, 1992

Rosa Parks with attorney Charles D. Langford at the Montgomery court-house during the bus boycott.

The Plan

The news of Parks's arrest spread fast. E. D. Nixon knew Rosa Parks. In every way, she was exactly the kind of person he had been looking for to act as the figurehead of the protest movement. Nixon contacted Rosa Parks immediately. He said that, with her permission, they could use her case to break down segregation on the buses. Parks didn't have to think very long. She said, "I'll go along with you, Mr. Nixon." A boycott of the Montgomery bus system in support of Parks was scheduled to start on Monday, December 5.

The Women's Political Council

In order for a boycott to be successful, everyone has to participate. Participation, however, depends on knowledge. In the 1950s, not everyone had televisions and telephones. There were no fax machines, cell phones, or e-mail. The quickest way to inform people of the boycott was by word of mouth.

The Women's Political Council, a group of professional black women in Montgomery, was responsible for spreading the word about the boycott. Its members stayed up late into the night making telephone calls and getting the message out through black neighborhoods. Without their efforts, the boycott might have been a dismal failure.

Jo Ann Robinson

One person who worked tirelessly to inform the black community about the upcoming boycott was Jo Ann Robinson. At the time, Robinson was the chairwoman of the Women's Political Council in Montgomery. Robinson spent the entire night of Thursday, December 1, 1955, printing up handbills urging people to boycott the buses on Monday, December 5. The following day, she distributed the flyers to black schools in Montgomery for students to take home to their parents.

Day One

As that first weekend in December 1955 came to an end, the protest's leaders asked themselves—would anyone in Montgomery actually boycott?

The question was there because it was not the first time that a boycott of the Montgomery bus system had been attempted. Once, a few years before the Rosa Parks incident, a minister named Vernon Johns had been riding a city bus and was told he had to give up his seat for a white passenger.

Negroes Have Rights, Too

"Negroes have rights, too, for if Negroes did not ride the buses, they could not operate. If we do not do something to stop these arrests, they will continue. The next time it may be you, or your daughter, or mother."

Jo Ann Robinson's flyer promoting the bus boycott, December 2, 1955

Women in Montgomery were eager for change in the segregation laws. They were responsible for spreading the word about the boycott and were active throughout the following year. In this picture, activist Ms. R. T. Adair speaks at a protest meeting during the boycott.

Reverend Johns tried to convince the other blacks on the bus to leave with him, but they stayed put. On the way out, an African-American man said to Reverend Johns, "You ought to know better."

There were many African Americans who might well be too frightened to protest because they knew there would be bad consequences. People were likely to be afraid of being fired by their white employers, or harassed on the streets, or worse. So there was good reason for the boycott's leaders to wonder just how many people would choose to participate.

Empty Buses

Buses are an everyday sight in any city. But the sight of an empty bus is rare. Imagine everyone's surprise when, on the morning of Monday, December 5, 1955, there were no black passengers on the Montgomery buses! Some buses that were used almost exclusively by African Americans were completely empty.

Montgomery did have a number of cab companies owned and operated by blacks. These cab companies offered to drive blacks to work for the same fare—ten cents—that they would have paid for a bus ride. On the morning of December 5, the cabs were packed and many people walked or rode bicycles to work, some for miles. The boycott was a success.

NEGRO BOYCOTT POSTER
This is one of the posters which city policemen yesterday removed from bus stop posts as Negroes staged a boycott against the Montgomery City Lines over arrest of a Negro woman on a transportation segregation charge. The poster states: "Remember we are fighting for a cause. Do not ride a bus today."

Several thousand Negroes use the buses on a normal day.

Police cars and motorcycles followed the buses periodically to prevent trouble after Sellers said some Negroes reported they were threatened with violence if they rode buses yesterday.

The circulars distributed in Negro residential districts Saturday urging the boycott yesterday in protest to the arrest of Rosa Parks were not signed. The Rev. A. W. Wilson, pastor of the Negro church where the meeting was to be held, said he would not disclose "under any circumstances" the names of those who asked permission to use the church for the meeting.

Ministers of various churches led the meeting last night.

Earlier, Bagley had issued a statement saying the bus company "is sorry if anyone expects us to be exempt from any state or city law."

In the Rosa Parks case yesterday, the city was prepared to offer testimony from 11 witnesses. Only three, Blake and two women passengers testified. One of the women said there was an empty seat where Rosa Parks could have sat if she had moved to the rear.

As the boycott started yesterday morning, Negroes stood on downtown street corners waiting for rides or piled into taxicabs. Many walked two or three miles to work in the crisp cold weather.

Most Negro children walked to school and there was a relay auto pickup system operating throughout most of the day.

This article appeared in the *Montgomery Advertiser* newspaper on December 6, 1955. It reports on the event and includes a picture of a poster that was used to promote the boycott in the African-American community.

Martin Luther King, Jr. (1929—1968)

Martin Luther King, Jr., grew up in a middle-class, black neighborhood in Atlanta, Georgia. Both his father and his mother's father were Baptist ministers, and King's early years were filled with religion. His reliance on faith grew as he became aware of racism and segregation.

King received a Ph.D. from Boston University in 1955 and had just become pastor at a Baptist church in Montgomery when the bus boycott began. After the boycott, King founded the Southern Christian Leadership Conference (SCLC) in 1957. Under King's leadership, the SCLC became influential in the civil rights movement with its nonviolent protests and work for voter registration among African Americans.

King is widely regarded to be the leader of the African-American civil rights movement. Among many activities, he led the March on Washington in 1963, a peaceful protest by over 200,000 people. King was awarded the Nobel Peace Prize in 1964 and continued to campaign against oppression, war, and poverty until his assassination in 1968.

The Montgomery Improvement Association

Black leaders in the community held a meeting at Holt Street Baptist Church that afternoon and evening. At the meeting, a new organization called the Montgomery Improvement Association (MIA) was formed. The man chosen to be the leader of this group was a minister named Martin Luther King, Jr.

King was an intelligent, passionate speaker. He was particularly influenced by the life and teachings of Mahatma Gandhi, a leader in India who developed a revolutionary form of peaceful protest. Gandhi encouraged strikes, boycotts, and protests, but he told his followers not to fight back against their enemies. This policy would be at the heart of the civil rights movement that was born that day.

The Boycott

Growing Strength

Originally, the boycott of the Montgomery bus system had no timetable. When black leaders met on the afternoon of December 5, 1955, they were not certain if the boycott should continue. Some thought that, although the boycott had been successful on that day, it might fall apart in the event of rain or if the police began harassing people.

Edward D. Nixon silenced these doubts. "What's the matter with you people?" he asked. "The time has come when you men are going to have to learn to be grown men or scared boys." After Nixon had finished, there was no question that the boycott would go on.

Nixon's speech was only the first of many important speeches that day. In the evening, Martin Luther King Jr. addressed the crowd. He asked the people repeatedly, "Do you want your freedom?" The reply, which grew in volume each time, was always "Yes!"

Ralph Abernathy, seen here during the bus boycott, presented three demands that would end segregation in Montgomery's transportation system. Abernathy later became King's right-hand man in the Southern Christian Leadership Conference and the group's leader after King's assassination in 1968.

Three Demands

The black community of Montgomery had decided to fight. Now it was time to make clear to the world, and particularly the white leaders of Montgomery, exactly what they were fighting for. Reverend Ralph Abernathy presented the crowd with a list of three demands to be made of the bus system.

First, black people wanted to be treated with respect on buses. Second, they wanted a policy of first-come, first-served seating. In other words, blacks would no longer be forced to give up their seats for white passengers. Third, they wanted blacks to be hired as bus drivers on the routes they traveled.

The crowd pledged its support and swore to continue the boycott until the list of demands had been met. It had been an amazing day and a thrilling evening. As everyone left the church that night, however, they all worried about the same thing—how would whites react to the boycott?

During the bus boycott, Martin Luther King, Jr. led the campaign for desegregation by calling attention to the cause of black Americans. This issue of *Liberation* magazine featured his story of the boycott on its cover.

White people resisted the boycott in numerous ways, including with intimidation. These Ku Klux Klan members strolled down a Montgomery street in November 1956 after being told they could not stage a full-scale march.

White Resistance

African Americans in Montgomery had good reason to worry. On December 8, King and members of the MIA met with city commissioners and representatives of the bus company. The MIA presented their three demands, but the bus company and government officials refused to cooperate.

In the coming months, the bus company and the government of Montgomery tried a number of different tactics to end the boycott. City Commissioner Clyde Sellers threatened that any cab driver found not charging the minimum forty-five cent fare would have to pay a hefty fine. The MIA responded to this threat by arranging for black car owners to drive groups of people to work.

City officials also tried to trick the black community into thinking that the boycott had ended. They leaked a story to the *Montgomery Advertiser* that the boycott was over. By this time, however, blacks in Montgomery were highly organized. Everyone was quickly informed that the boycott was still on.

We Are Tired

"We are here this evening to say to those who have mistreated us so long that we are tired—tired of being segregated and humiliated, tired of being kicked about by the brutal feet of oppression."

Martin Luther King, Jr., speaking to the crowd at Holt Street Baptist Church , December 5, 1955

Tension and Violence

By January 1956, the bus company was suffering greatly from the loss of business. Store owners in downtown Montgomery were losing money because blacks never came into town to shop anymore.

The city found more ways to make life difficult for the boycotters. White women who had begun driving their black maids to and from work were arrested for speeding. Black people who chose to walk to work were arrested for loitering.

Rolling Churches

When black cab companies were fined by the city for offering cheap rides to their customers, the MIA purchased a number of station wagons that became their own unofficial cab company. Members of the MIA called these station wagons "rolling churches."

City officials of Montgomery tried to break up the taxi service arranged by the MIA. If they could do this, blacks would be forced to use the city buses to get to work. At one point, city officials attempted to get the insurance policies for the MIA cars cancelled. This failed when King made arrangements for car insurance with a black insurance agent in Atlanta.

The Holt Street Baptist Church station wagon, now on display in the Rosa Parks Museum with model figures showing a boycott scene.

On January 30, King's home was bombed. The violence would continue just two days later with the bombing of Nixon's home. Still, the boycott continued

Frustrated and angry, the white leaders of Montgomery chose to take advantage of an old regulation outlawing boycotts. On February 21, 1956, about ninety blacks, including King, were arrested for breaking this law. It was a bold move that only succeeded in gaining more publicity for the movement. King was fined $500, but his popularity and that of the boycotters rose greatly. The protest gained support all around the country.

The Lawsuit

The resolve of the black community was unbreakable. As the cold winter turned into a stormy spring, the boycott went on. The black community leaders knew that it would be difficult to get the bus company and city officials to meet their demands, however. They realized that their best hope for success was in the courts. Back in February 1956, one of Montgomery's few black lawyers, a man named Fred Gray, had filed a lawsuit on behalf of the MIA, charging that bus segregation was unconstitutional.

No Victory Allowed

"If we granted the Negroes these demands, they would go about boasting of a victory that they had won over the white people, and this we will not stand for."

Montgomery City Commissioner Clyde Sellers

A crowd gathers outside the city courthouse where about ninety citizens were being tried for boycotting. Nothing, not even arrests, could break the boycott once the black people of Montgomery were united in their effort.

In May 1956, this case was heard before a **federal** District Court. The MIA lawyers argued that bus segregation violated the Fourteenth Amendment. The Fourteenth Amendment clearly states that "No State shall make or enforce any law which shall abridge the privileges or **immunities** of citizens of the United States." On June 4, the District Court ruled in favor of the MIA. The city of Montgomery decided to appeal the decision to the Supreme Court.

A Small Victory for Racism

Someone in city government had noticed that the people who depended on the MIA station wagons for transportation would gather at specific points in the city to be picked up. In October 1956, Montgomery's Mayor Gayle requested a **restraining order** against these groups, claiming that they were singing loudly and disturbing the peace.

Tuesday, November 13, 1956, was an important day for Mayor Gayle. He was granted his restraining order. It was a small victory that was quickly overshadowed by a much more important event.

The Montgomery bus boycott inspired others to fight segregation. In Tallahassee, Florida, a passenger is being dropped off at a downtown pick-up and drop-off point during a boycott of the bus system in June 1956. It was gathering places such as this that Mayor Gayle targeted with a restraining order in Montgomery.

The Supreme Court

The Constitution lists all of the basic laws of the United States. The task of the Supreme Court is to interpret the United States Constitution and see that U.S. laws comply with it.

The members of the Supreme Court include a Chief Justice and an unspecified number of Associate Justices (usually there are eight). The Supreme Court hears about two hundred cases a year. In the Supreme Court, there are no witnesses and no jury. Arguments from both sides of a case are heard, and then the justices meet in private to discuss the case. Rulings are decided by a majority vote.

A Huge Victory for Equal Rights

As fate would have it, the Supreme Court decision was announced on the same day. The Supreme Court ruled in favor of the MIA, deciding that segregation on buses was unconstitutional.

The reaction to the Supreme Court decision was ecstatic. People cried and hugged and cheered. The evening of November 13, a celebration was held at Holt Street Baptist Church. King delivered a stirring speech, saying, "We must not take this as a victory over the white man but as a victory for justice and democracy."

On December 21, 1956, Martin Luther King took a seat on a Montgomery bus next to Glenn Smiley, a white minister from Texas. Officially, segregation on public transportation was over.

The Mandate

The Supreme Court decision was not enough to make the blacks return immediately to the buses. Everyone decided to wait until proof of the Supreme Court **mandate** had arrived. The boycotters wanted to see it in writing.

The mandate finally arrived on Thursday, December 20, 1956. The next day, December 21, a number of MIA members including Nixon and King boarded a Montgomery bus. Their bus ride received a lot of media attention. By comparison, Rosa Parks's first bus ride in over a year was a quiet event. When Parks sat down, however, she could do so knowing she had achieved her right as a U.S. citizen to sit where she chose.

A Remarkable Achievement

"The bus protest carried on by the colored people of Montgomery, Alabama, without violence, has been one of the most remarkable achievements of people fighting for their own rights, but doing so without bloodshed and with the most remarkable restraint and discipline, that we have ever witnessed in this country."

Eleanor Roosevelt, civil rights campaigner and widow of President Franklin D. Roosevelt

The Civil Rights Movement

After the Boycott

There is a story told about those first days after the end of the boycott. A white bus passenger noticed two blacks sitting in front of him and said, "I see this isn't going to be a white Christmas." One of the black passengers turned to see that the white man was smiling. The black man answered, "That's right." The crowd on the bus laughed.

Not all white people accepted the change so easily. Unfortunately, **integration** was a slow, difficult process. Gunshots were heard in Montgomery with increasing frequency. One pregnant black woman was shot in the leg while riding a bus.

Another victim of racism was Reverend Ralph Abernathy, the man who had originally read the list of three demands on the first night of the boycott. Reverend Abernathy's home and church were bombed. Another four black churches and the homes of two other black pastors were also bombed. Everyone was very scared, and for good reason.

On January 9, 1957, just a couple of weeks after the end of the bus boycott, the African-American Bell Street Baptist church in Montgomery was bombed in an act of racial violence. The city suspended bus services on January 10.

Doing Nothing

Some of this violence must be blamed on the Montgomery city officials. The MIA took care to issue rules and guidelines in order to ensure that the integration of the bus lines went smoothly. City officials, on the other hand, did nothing. They made no effort to give the general public a clear idea of how to integrate peacefully.

This was not the result of bad planning or incompetence. Rather, city officials wanted and even hoped for violence. It was their way of punishing the black community. They took particular delight in suspending bus services when violence became a concern. They enjoyed the fact that by stopping the buses, they could force black people to walk.

Do Not Strike Back

"If cursed, do not curse back. If pushed, do not push back. If struck, do not strike back, but evidence love and goodwill at all times."

From an MIA publication on how to integrate peacefully

The Little Rock Nine

Little Rock student Elizabeth Eckford walks to school while white citizens of Little Rock pursue her and shout abuse.

The first significant civil rights victory after Montgomery took place in Little Rock, Arkansas, where Central High School was supposed to be fully integrated at the start of school in September 1957. However, Arkansas's governor Orval Faubus called on the National Guard to prevent nine black children who were slated to attend Central High from entering the building. In response, President Dwight D. Eisenhower arranged for federal troops to escort the "Little Rock Nine" to school.

The Civil Rights Movement

In a way, however, the anger barely mattered. The Supreme Court's decision had made history. The success of the boycott was the start of a chain reaction that would transform the entire nation.

The African-American civil rights movement was at its peak from about 1955 to 1965. During that time, blacks and whites worked together in a variety of ways to bring an end to segregation. Under the leadership of Martin Luther King and others, they continued to use the policy of non-violent protest that had been so effective in Montgomery.

Sit-Ins

By this time, organizations like the NAACP and the Southern Christian Leadership Conference were teaching young blacks all over America the many ways they could fight discrimination. Young men and women were eager to get involved in the movement and prove themselves.

Students in Greensboro, North Carolina, sit at a whites-only lunch counter. The students were ignored by staff and abused by white customers.

On February 1, 1960, four students staged a **sit-in** at a Woolworth's store in Greensboro, North Carolina. The men sat at the whites-only lunch counter of the store and, because they were black, they were not served. When the store closed that evening, the students left. They came back day after day until their peaceful protest caught the attention of the nation.

Soon, other sit-ins were taking place at stores and other public facilities in several states. The first proof that sit-ins were effective came on May 10, 1960, when the city of Nashville, Tennessee, began desegregating its public facilities.

In 1961, a bus carrying freedom riders prepares to leave the bus station in Montgomery for Jackson, Mississippi. Because of attacks by white people, the National Guard and state troops were present. The bus was escorted by sixteen highway patrol cars as it left the city.

Freedom Rides

Sit-ins were not a new idea. They had taken place in American cities as early as 1943. The ability to give old ideas new life, however, was one of the civil rights movement's greatest assets. Another old idea was the "freedom ride." Back in 1947, the Supreme Court had ruled that segregation on interstate buses and trains was unconstitutional. After that ruling, members of the Congress of Racial Equality (CORE) rode these buses and trains to see if the law would be upheld. They were bullied and even arrested.

In 1961, CORE decided it was time to repeat this test. On May 4, 1961, a group of thirteen CORE members began a journey from Washington, D.C., through the South to New Orleans. Upon entering Alabama, their buses were attacked. People threw stones and firebombs and slashed the buses' tires. Some of the riders were injured. The Attorney General at that time was Robert Kennedy, brother of the president. He arranged for federal marshals to escort freedom riders.

The March on Washington

In 1963, civil rights leaders decided to organize a march to Washington, D.C., to support the Civil Rights Act. If passed by Congress, this bill would outlaw racial discrimination in public places and make provisions for equal employment and education opportunities.

More than 200,000 people marched on the nation's capital on August 28, 1963. The highlight of the March on Washington came when Martin Luther King, Jr., delivered a moving speech about his dream for the future.

The Civil Rights Act

The Civil Rights Act was signed by President Lyndon Johnson on July 2, 1964. By this time, the civil rights movement had achieved

President Lyndon Johnson, front at desk, signs the Civil Rights Act of 1964. In the South, however, African Americans were still prevented from voting.

Over 25,000 people gather at the State Capitol building in Montgomery Alabama, in 1965. The Confederate flag flies under the state flag on top of the Capitol dome. The Confederate flag was used as a symbol of resistance against black civil rights.

Free At Last

". . . all God's children, black men and white men, Jews and gentiles, Protestants and Catholics, will be able to join hands and sing in the words of the old Negro spiritual: 'Free at last. Free at last. . . .'"

Martin Luther King, Jr., August 28, 1963

a great deal, but many blacks were still unable to exercise one of their most basic rights: voting. In order to vote, a person must first register, but blacks in the South were often prevented from registering. Other **legislation**, like the 1957 Civil Rights Act, tried to increase the number of black registrants but actually did very little.

Selma

One city where registering to vote was a particular problem was Selma, Alabama. For seven weeks in January and February 1965, a protest was held in Selma. During a nighttime march, Selma police shot to death a young black man named Jimmie Lee Jackson. Jackson's death resulted in a protest march from Selma all the way to Montgomery. By the time it reached Montgomery on March 25, the crowd had grown to more than 25,000 people. The rally held that day on the steps of the state capitol seemed to bring the civil rights movement full circle. Even Rosa Parks was there.

Later that year, on August 6, President Johnson signed the Voting Rights Act of 1965. The law prohibits discrimination in voting practices or procedures because of race and color. This stands as one of the civil rights movement's greatest achievements.

Conclusion

Honoring the Civil Rights Heroes

Martin Luther King, Jr., was assassinated on April 4, 1968, in Memphis, Tennessee. While King's murder serves as a bitter reminder of the evil of racism, his legacy remains. As his friend Ralph Abernathy noted, "The grave is too narrow for his soul." In his honor, Martin Luther King, Jr. Day is celebrated every January on the Monday nearest his January 15 birthday.

To honor everyone else—all of the black heroes before, during, and after the civil rights movement—Black History Month is celebrated every February. That month was chosen because a number of important events in black history have taken place in February.

Rosa Parks

Rosa Parks, ninety years old in 2003, has received many honors and awards. On June 15, 1999, Parks was awarded the Congressional Gold Medal. During her short speech, Parks said, "This medal is encouragement for all of us to continue until all have rights."

On December 1, 2000, forty-five years after the Montgomery bus boycott, Troy State University in Montgomery opened the Rosa Parks Library and Museum. The museum tells the story of the Montgomery bus boycott and ensures that Parks's memory will live on.

The Lorraine Motel in Memphis, Tennessee, site of Martin Luther King's murder, is now the National Civil Rights Museum. King was shot when he stepped onto the motel balcony above where the two cars are parked.

Inequality Continues

According to a survey in 2000, whites in Montgomery are 48.8 percent of the population, while black Americans are 48.6 percent. Other ethnic groups in the city have populations that are growing daily. Clearly, people of all races are learning to live together in Montgomery.

There is still a long way to go, however. Freedom is now taken for granted, thanks to the abolitionists of the 1800s. Voting rights are extended to all citizens, thanks to the civil rights activists of the 1900s. But African Americans and other minority groups, although growing in population, are still poorer than white people and not as visible in politics and other areas of influence in the United States.

A sculpture of Rosa Parks is displayed in the Civil Rights Institute in Birmingham, Alabama. It commemorates Parks's historic bus journey in December 1955.

The Legacy of the Montgomery Bus Boycott

In the years following the success of the Montgomery bus boycott, the civil rights movement, although present ever since the days of slavery, found a stronger voice in American society.

Later, other victims of discrimination would find strength in numbers. Protest movements that led peaceful campaigns for basic human rights and other reforms included women's liberation, the antiwar movement, the gay rights movement, and the environmental movement. Each of these movements has affected the thinking of Americans and the actions of government leaders.

Time Line

1619	First Africans are brought to America and sold as slaves.
1641	Massachusetts recognizes slavery as a legal institution.
1860	Abraham Lincoln is elected president.
1861	February: Confederate States of America is formed by rebel southern states.
	April 12: Civil War begins.
1863	January 1: Emancipation Proclamation goes into effect.
1865	April 9: Confederate surrender ends Civil War.
	December 18: Thirteenth Amendment is approved.
	Reconstruction period begins.
	Ku Klux Klan is founded.
1877	Reconstruction period ends.
1896	Supreme Court rules in *Plessy v. Ferguson*.
1909	February: NAACP is founded.
1913	February 4: Birth of Rosa (McCauley) Parks.
1929	January 15: Birth of Martin Luther King, Jr.
1954	Supreme Court rules in *Brown v. Board of Education*.
1955	August: Murder of Emmett Till.
	December 1: Rosa Parks refuses to give up her bus seat.
	December 5: Montgomery bus boycott begins.
1956	November 13: Supreme Court outlaws segregation on buses.
	December 21: Montgomery bus boycott ends.
1957	Southern Christian Leadership Conference is founded.
	September: Integration of Little Rock Central High School, Arkansas.
1960	February 1: First sit-in takes place in Greensboro, North Carolina.
1961	May 4: Freedom rides to southern cities begin.
1963	August 28: March on Washington.
1964	July 2: Civil Rights Act is signed.
1965	March 25: Protest march from Selma, Alabama, reaches Montgomery.
	August 6: Voting Rights Act is signed.
1967	Thurgood Marshall is appointed as first black Supreme Court justice.
1968	April 4: Assassination of Martin Luther King, Jr.
1999	June 15: Rosa Parks receives Congressional Gold Medal.
2000	December 1: Rosa Parks Library and Museum opens in Montgomery.

Glossary

activist: person who takes action in support of or in protest against issues in his or her society.

Amendment: official change or addition made to the United States Constitution.

boycott: refusal to do business with a particular business in protest against its policies.

civil rights: basic rights—such as freedom of movement, voting, ownership of property, education, and choice of religion and political beliefs—of every person.

class action: lawsuit brought by one or more persons representing a large group of people.

colony: settlement, area, or country owned or controlled by another nation.

desegregate: get rid of segregation.

economy: system of producing and distributing goods and services.

emancipation: freeing of enslaved African Americans.

federal: having to do with the whole nation rather than separate states.

immunity: protection from an outside force, such as the law.

indentured: contracted arrangement between employer and worker in which the worker agrees to work for a period of time.

integration: mixing together, as when schools were desegregated.

jurisdiction: area of authority to govern or say how something should be done.

lawsuit: case brought before a court of law for decision.

legislation: deciding and enacting of laws.

mandate: order by a court to say how something must be done.

racist: having opinions about a person based on race rather than on true qualities.

Reconstruction: rebuilding. The Reconstruction period after the Civil War was a time when some leaders tried to rebuild the South and change U.S. attitudes.

reform: change in society intended to improve conditions.

restraining order: order by a court limiting a person's movements or location. In Montgomery, the court order would be used by city officials to stop people from gathering to wait for the MIA taxi service.

secede: withdraw from the Union.

segregation: separation of people of different races.

sit-in: protest in which people seat themselves in a place and refuse to move.

Supreme Court: highest court in the United States, with the power to make final decisions on matters of law and interpretation of the U.S. Constitution.

unconstitutional: action or law that goes against the principles of the U.S. Constitution.

Union: United States of America. The term is mostly used to describe the United States during the Civil War after the southern states seceded.

U.S. Territory: geographical area that belongs to and is governed by the United States but is not included in any of its states.

Further Information

Books

Fremon, David K. *The Jim Crow Laws and Racism in American History*. Enslow, 2000.

Levine, Ellen. *Freedom's Children: Young Civil Rights Activists Tell Their Own Stories*. Puffin, 2000.

Parks, Rosa. *I Am Rosa Parks*. Penguin, 1997.

Rhym, Darren. *The NAACP* (African American Achievers). Chelsea House, 2001.

Sanders, Mark. *The Supreme Court*. Steadwell Books/Raintree Steck-Vaughn, 2000.

Web Sites

www.ferris.edu/jimcrow/menu.htm The Jim Crow Museum at Ferris State University seeks to explain racism and racial stereotyping through its online exhibition.

www.tsum.edu/museum The Rosa Parks Library and Museum at Troy State University in Montgomery has online exhibit about the Montgomery bus boycott and lots of information about Rosa Parks and her achievements.

www.naacp.org The web site of the National Association for the Advancement of Colored People offers historical information and current news about African-American civil rights.

Useful Addresses

Rosa Parks Library and Museum
251 Montgomery Street
Montgomery, AL 36104
Telephone: (334) 241-8615

Index

Page numbers in *italics* indicate maps and diagrams. Page numbers in **bold** indicate other illustrations.